World More Beautiful

The Life and Art of Barbara Cooney

For the women in my life
who make things and, in doing so,
make the world more beautiful —A.B.K.

For the love of illustration
and a life spent making art —B.S.

Text copyright © 2024 by Angela Burke Kunkel
Jacket art and interior illustrations copyright © 2024 by Becca Stadtlander

Visit us on the Web! rhcbooks.com

Educators and librarians, for a variety of teaching tools, visit us at RHTeachersLibrarians.com

Library of Congress Cataloging-in-Publication Data is available upon request.
ISBN 978-0-593-48438-8 (trade) — ISBN 978-0-593-48439-5 (lib. bdg.) — ISBN 978-0-593-48440-1 (ebook)

The illustrations for this book were created with gouache.
The text is set in 15-point Bembo MT Pro.
Interior design by Rachael Cole

MANUFACTURED IN CHINA
10 9 8 7 6 5 4 3 2 1
First Edition

World More Beautiful
The Life and Art of Barbara Cooney

written by angela burke kunkel illustrated by becca stadtlander

RANDOM HOUSE STUDIO ⌂ NEW YORK

From the top of the Hotel Bossert is a view of both
the city and the sea.

Barbara is born in Room 1127, along with her
twin brother. A boy and a girl. A mother and a father.

The men in Barbara's family understand lumber, and ships, and money. Her father studies the stock market, numbers ticking steadily away in black and white.

But Barbara and her mother love art, and color, and light.

Barbara's favorite days are when she stays home sick in bed and gets to paint and draw. Her mother offers all her own things—pencils and paper, palettes and paints. No lessons, no rules, except to keep her brushes clean.

In the summers, they leave the city for the sea, where Barbara scrambles among the rocks, wind whipping her hair, light sparkling on the water. Summer is gray, and blue, and green, and free.

Summer is Maine.

Yet summers turn to autumns, and it is back to school, facts
laid out in black and white. And, like a season, childhood turns,
too. And pretty soon, Barbara is grown up.

Barbara goes out into the world with a portfolio full of color, thinking she might like to illustrate books. She meets with publisher after publisher, looking for work.

With work comes rules:

Scratchboard.

Precise, exacting.

Small.

Unforgiving.

No room for mistakes.

She scratches steadily away in black and white, because there are houses to heat and children to feed, and because an editor tells her she has no color sense. But Barbara loves the world, and all the colors in it.

At home, when she is not at her desk, Barbara walks the woods with her children, pointing out strange mosses, lichens, witch hazel.

One evening, she stops at the barnyard door, struck by the beauty of a rooster in a certain slant of light. Ideas take shape while Barbara is sick in bed, just like when she was little.

White pages fill—a rooster and chickens,
a farm and children, animals and growing
things. The publisher allows for five simple
colors. The book is a huge success. Because
Barbara has drawn all this for *herself*.

And that is when Barbara

begins

to break

the rules,

to scratch the surface of what she can do.

Because life

isn't laid out

in black

and white.

YELLOW-GREEN · LIGHT GREEN · MOSS GREEN · MEDIUM GREEN · EMERALD GREEN · NEUTRAL BLUE

LIGHT TAN · DARK TAN · DARK BROWN · GREY · WHITE · BLACK

Barbara journeys to faraway places, to see stories in living color.
She takes her family to France, and while wandering the market,
shopping for groceries, she studies the peachy pinks of stucco houses,
the ochres of tiled roofs. She hikes up a mountainside with her
children, and finds a landscape that looks like a lullaby.

Barbara climbs up Mount Olympus in Greece, to see
what the gods might see. And she explores a cave down
by the sea, to see what sailors might see, too. Sapphire
and cerulean, azure and ultramarine.

In Mexico, there are big mountains, an even bigger sky. There is red adobe, the purple arches of jacaranda trees, pink prickly pear, the silvery green of aloe and agave.

Barbara drives a yellow Volkswagen across a brown
landscape, soaking up sun, and color, and light.

She packs everything she might ever need. Thirteen pieces of luggage; a camera, film, sketchbooks, even a snakebite kit. She brings it all home, and more, too—wildflowers pressed between pages, a silk kimono, tiny paintings of saints on tin— and those become her palette, her colors, her books.

Because always, Maine calls her home, every summer, with its blue and purple and rose-colored flowers. Barbara is moving slower. Her back hurts. Bags feel heavier.

It is time to build a little house by the sea.

In that house, her hair graying, Barbara begins to paint her own life—fields and headlands, islands and skies, grandfathers and little girls. Which she was, once.

Barbara is an old woman now. And even with all of her books, all of her children and grandchildren, a home in the place she loves best—there is still one thing she must do.

In the center of town, there is a cramped clapboard house. Its carpet is worn.
The stairs creak. The roof leaks. It's been the library for as long as anyone can remember.

But Barbara can picture a spacious room, full of color and light, where children
wander the shelves, looking for stories of faraway places.

On a summer evening, there is a gentle breeze and a party out on a lawn, by a river that flows to the sea. People are here to buy art from the books they love—small pen-and-inks, big bright canvases, some by Barbara and some by others. Every picture, every page, will help to build a new library. Barbara weaves among the crowd, a white braid her crown, and passes sparklers to every guest.

The moon rises, the night grows dark. The party lasts late into the night.

Barbara will not be there to see the ground broken, or the first bricks laid. Except, maybe, she is.

A life is more than a timeline, dates set down in black and white.

There are harsh winters and soft springs, tides that follow the moon, rivers that flow to the sea. There are blue and purple and rose-colored flowers, more and more of them, year after year.

Pages turn. We reach the end.

Books close, then open again.

We do not always know the next story.

But we know it could be beautiful.

Author's Note

Barbara Cooney was born on August 6, 1917, in Brooklyn Heights, at the Hotel Bossert. The hotel was built by her grandfather Louis Bossert, a prominent New York lumber merchant. Growing up as the only girl in the family was often a lonely experience for Cooney, as her father, Russell Schenck Cooney, tended to favor her three brothers. Thankfully, she and her mother, Mae Bossert Cooney, connected over their love of art. An artist herself, Mae encouraged her daughter's talent by sharing brushes and paints.

Cooney was raised on Long Island but spent summers in Waldoboro, Maine, establishing a lifelong connection to the people and places along the seacoast that became the inspiration for many books throughout her career.

After graduating in 1938 from Smith College, where she worried that the limited studio art classes did not strengthen her skills, Cooney attended the Art Students League of New York like her mother before her. (Mae's artistic journey was later fictionalized by Cooney in *Hattie and the Wild Waves*.) Cooney concentrated on etching and lithography, with the hope of illustrating children's books.

Barbara Cooney

Her first book as an illustrator, *Åke and His World* by Bertil Malmberg, was published in 1940. Cooney's debut as an author-illustrator, *King of Wreck Island*, came out the following year. Skilled in a medium known as scratchboard—where the artist meticulously draws images by scratching on drawing board with sharp instruments—Cooney took on project after project working in black and white. Although she desired to do something different, financial necessity dictated that she take the work offered to her.

By the time Cooney won the Caldecott Medal for *Chanticleer and the Fox* in 1959, she had illustrated over forty books. The award opened up opportunities to experiment more broadly. From the 1960s onward, Cooney not only began to work more in color, but explored faraway places, using details from her trips to inform her work. Cooney's many travels included a stay in France for an edition of *Mother Goose,* a trip to Greece for a series of tales by Homer, and journeys through Mexico for collections of Spanish-language nursery rhymes and folktales. Her time in North Africa and Oceania is depicted in the pages of her best-known work, *Miss Rumphius.*

Like Miss Rumphius, Cooney found herself returning to Maine after her extensive travels, building a home on the Damariscotta River. These years marked another shift in her career. She won a second Caldecott for *Ox-Cart Man* in 1980, then worked on her most personal trilogy: *Miss Rumphius* (1982), *Island Boy* (1988), and *Hattie and the Wild Waves* (1990). In a 1995 essay, Cooney called these three works "as close to any autobiography as I will ever get."

Barbara Cooney also left a legacy beyond her career as an author and illustrator, which spanned sixty years and 110 books, with her efforts to help build a new library in Damariscotta. In addition to her own financial contributions, she organized an auction of work from other well-known illustrators (Eric Carle, Tomie dePaola, Trina Schart Hyman, Jerry Pinkney, and Maurice Sendak, to name a few) to raise more funds and encourage others to give. Although Cooney died at the age of eighty-two on March 10, 2000, about a month before the ground was broken to build the new library, her presence could be felt throughout the project—from the lupines schoolchildren painted on construction fencing to a photograph of Cooney that sits above the shelves in the children's room today. To borrow a simple phrase from her beloved *Miss Rumphius,* Barbara Cooney left the world more beautiful.

Illustrations from books by Barbara Cooney: *Miss Rumphius, Island Boy,* and *Hattie and the Wild Waves* (from left to right).

Selected Bibliography

Cooney, Barbara. "Caldecott Award Acceptance." In *Newbery and Caldecott Medal Books: 1956–1965,* edited by Lee Kingman. Boston: Horn Book, 1965.

Cooney, Barbara. "Caldecott Medal Acceptance." In *Newbery and Caldecott Medal Books: 1976–1985,* edited by Lee Kingman. Boston: Horn Book, 1986.

Dougherty, Joanna Foster, film director. *The Lively Art of Picture Books.* Norwalk, CT: Weston Woods Studios, 1964.

Frelinghuysen, Alice Cooney. "Travels with Hattie and Eleanor: Researching Biography with Barbara Cooney." Lecture at Bowdoin College, August 6, 2016.

Perl-Rosenthal, Nathan. "Children's Books for Uncertain Times." *The Atlantic,* December 2017.

Porter, Barnaby, and Susan Porter. Personal interview, March 26, 2021, and July 1, 2022.

Porter, Phoebe. Personal interview, March 18, 2021.

Acknowledgments

A special thank-you to Barnaby and Susan Porter, as well as Phoebe Porter, for their generosity and willingness to share stories and memories of Barbara Cooney Porter. Thank you also to Terry Hapach and the staff at the Skidompha Public Library in Damariscotta, Maine, for their invaluable research assistance.

Afterword

I was fortunate to have known Barbara Cooney better than most. For over half a century, she was my mother—a pretty tough job when I and my brother and sisters were acting up, but she was good at it. She had an amusing saying: "Kids are like pancakes. The first few don't always turn out so well." I was one of the first; she had her work cut out for her. But I like to think she succeeded admirably, opening our eyes as kids to what was important in this world.

When she wrote the story of *Miss Rumphius,* with its basic message *We must all do something to make the world more beautiful,* she felt it was a deeply important lesson that all the world's children should take to heart. By *something,* she meant more than simply planting flowers or making beautiful pictures—far more. For her it meant living graciously, being kind and friendly to all people and animals, being generous, taking good care of the world around you, helping out when something needs doing . . . and even just trying to be very good at whatever it is you hope to do in your life, so that you can smile and be happy. That smile and happiness, all by itself, will make the world more beautiful.

—Barnaby Porter